# Scrap

Written by Jan Burchett
and Sara Vogler

Illustrated by George Black

## Collins

I am Scrap. I think rubbish spoils this planet. Too much rubbish is dumped in tips.

Plastic floats on to the sand, spoiling the coast.

# Things we can do

Help me clear up this planet.
Sort rubbish into the proper bins.

Put brown, green and clear jars in this bin. They get turned into fresh jars.

We can all help clear up rubbish on the coast.

# It is not just us!

This insect clears up dung. It turns brown dung into nests and food.

**Fun fact**
Dung is poo!

When the hermit crab needs a bigger shell, a little crab starts living in the shell that is left.

This nest is full of rubbish. Bright sparkling rubbish is selected to construct the nest.

# We can transform rubbish into fun objects

Plastic spoons and lids were transformed into this bright dress and hat!

**Remember**
Drop rubbish in the proper bins or turn it into fun objects!

An artist cleared up plastic rubbish and turned it into this fantastic shark!

Plastic containers were transformed into this boat.

We can transform card into a painted cabin or monster or an eggbox croc.

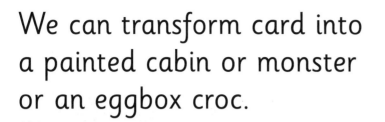

**Fun fact**
Jars can be paint pots and flower pots.

# Eggbox croc

egg boxes

paint brush

red paint

green paint

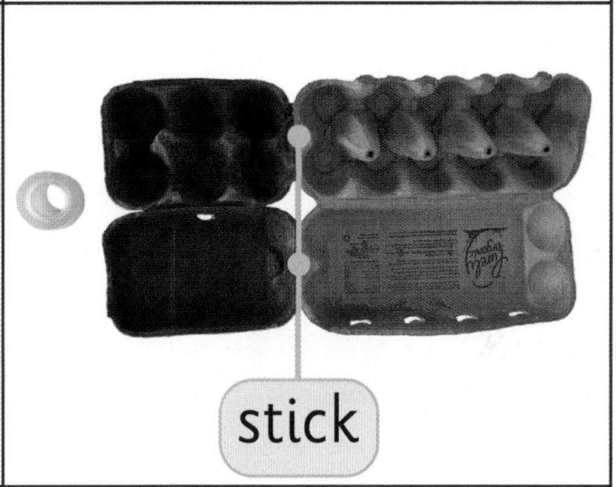

stick

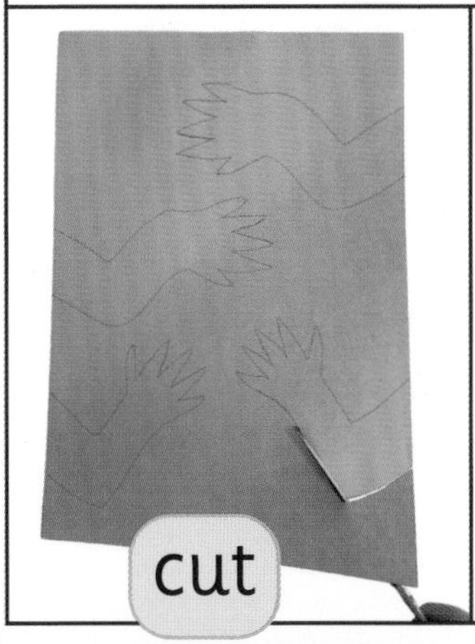

cut

13

# Sorting scrap

# 🐾 Review: After reading 🐾

Use your assessment from hearing the children read to choose any GPCs, words or tricky words that need additional practice.

## Read 1: Decoding

- Remind children to use the chunking method to help them to sound words out.
    - o Point to **transformed** on page 10, and show them how to chunk this word. (***trans/formed***)
    - o Repeat for **containers** and **fantastic** on page 11. (***con/tain/ers, fan/tas/tic***)
    - o Let children choose other words to read in the same way.
- Point to shorter words with adjacent consonants, such as **scrap**, **spoils**, **coast** (pages 2 and 3). Say: Can you blend in your head when you read these words aloud?

## Read 2: Prosody

- Model reading pages 8 and 9 to the children as if you are Scrap presenting a programme about planet Earth on television.
- Discuss how you can hold a listener's attention. (e.g. *emphasis for interesting words, change of tone to surprise*)
- Ask the children to take turns reading a sentence. Ask listeners to think about whether the text sounds interesting.

## Read 3: Comprehension

- Discuss what the children have done, or hope to do, to clear up rubbish or help sort it out.
- Ask: What sort of book is this? Does it contain information or does it tell a story? Discuss how it gives information, although it uses a character – Scrap – as the narrator.
- Point to the word **proper** on page 4. Ask: What are proper bins? (e.g. *bins for sorting, bins for collection*) What is an example of a proper bin? (e.g. *the green bin in the photo*)
- Turn to pages 14 and 15, and focus on the sequence of events for each type of rubbish. Refer back to pages 4 and 5, if necessary. Ask:
    - o How is the scrap sorted?
    - o What goes in each bin? What other things could go into each bin?
    - o What can the newspaper/can/plastic bottle be made into?